I0482118

PREPARING TAX RETURNS FOR MINISTERS:
An Easy Reference Guide

By:

Kay K. Mortimer, EA
Original publication by Lighthouse Publishing of the Carolinas
Reprinted 2017.

CHAPTER ONE

The Unique Challenge of Ministers' Taxes

Ministers sit in a unique seat when it comes to their tax reporting requirements. As a dual-status taxpayer, ministers require proper tax handling of items pertaining particularly to them.

Tax professionals should be aware that, in many cases, churches use volunteers to function as treasurers. Such volunteers, in many cases, are unfamiliar with tax law and the implications of tax treatment for items pertaining to their ministerial staff.

Tax professionals who learn the correct handling of ministers' taxes set themselves apart from average tax preparers unskilled in this arena. So, who is a "minister?"

Definition of Minister

Pastors, rabbis, priests, and other religious leaders of churches wear the collective title of "minister" in the eyes of the IRS. The official definition says ministers are "individuals who are duly ordained, commissioned, or licensed by a religious body constituting a church or church denomination."[1]

The IRS further explains that they "can conduct religious worship, perform sacerdotal functions, and administer the specific ordinances or sacraments of their church or denomination."[2]

For simplification purposes, the term "minister" shall be used collectively to refer to any individual meeting the definition of a "minister" for purposes of tax law.

Ministers fall into an unusual category known as "dual-status" taxpayers. This means that, for SECA (self-employed social security and Medicare) purposes, they are considered self-employed, while for federal tax purposes they generally are considered common-law employees. How their earnings are treated, and which earnings are taxable for which type of tax, is the challenge for the tax professional.

[1]Publication 517: *Social Security and Other Information for Members of the Clergy and Religious Workers,* Department of the Treasury, Internal Revenue Service, p.3.

[2]Ibid, p. 3.

The following excerpt helps to clarify the definition of a minister:

> ### How the Courts Have Ruled
> Court action in 1989 established 5 factors when determining whether one is a minister for tax purposes.
> 1. Does the individual administer the sacraments?
> 2. Does the individual conduct worship services?
> 3. Does the individual perform services in the "control, conduct, or maintenance of a religious organization" under the authority of a church denomination or religious denomination?
> 4. Is the individual "ordained, commissioned, or licensed?"
> 5. Is the individual considered a spiritual leader by his or her religious body?

If you meet some but not all of these factors, the IRS may or may not consider you a minister. Under the 1989 tax court case, not all factors had to be satisfied. It should be noted that only factor 4, that one be "licensed, ordained, or commissioned," needs to be present in *every* case. The more of the remaining criteria that one can meet, the more likely one is to fulfill the definition of "minister of the Gospel." (However, some more-recent court cases and an IRS Private Letter Ruling have required that all factors be satisfied. Nevertheless, according to leading church law experts, the 1989 case is still viable precedent. The Income Tax Regulations noted previously remain the reliable source for determining ministerial qualification.) Also, the Tax Court *has not* recognized persons as ministers for tax purposes solely on the basis that they were licensed in order to gain tax benefits. In other words, if one seeks a district license or ordination simply to gain tax benefits rather than the rights and privileges associated with it, then the IRS likely would not view that individual as a minister for tax purposes.

How the Rules Are Applied

Generally, there are two "qualifications" for recognition as a minister for tax purposes: (1) a proper credentialing which gives one the *ability to perform* certain services in the exercise of ministry; and (2) the *actual performance* of services in the exercise of the individual's ministry.

First of all, the individual must be recognized by the denomination as one authorized to do the work of ministry (preach the Word, conduct worship, administer the sacraments, perform marriages). The IRS and the Tax Courts would understand this to be one duly ordained, licensed, or commissioned...

Second, the minister must perform tasks which qualify him or her for tax benefits (conduct worship; preach the Word; administer the sacraments; direct, manage, or promote in order to maintain the religious organization; work in an integral agency of the denomination to control, direct, or manage that institution;

or be assigned by the denomination to a specific task).[3]

Ministers who've taken a Vow of Poverty

For ministers of orders who <u>have</u> taken a "vow of poverty," their earnings are considered the earnings of the religious order, and are therefore, not "income" to them. In this case, they receive special treatment as to both federal and self-employment tax (SE) reporting.

Chapter Two

Determining a Minister's Employment Status

A determination must be made as to a minister's employment status: common-law employee or self-employed independent contractor. In most cases, ministers who are paid a regular salary to conduct religious services for a church are considered common-law employees of that church.

This is generally true because one of the key deciding factors between employees versus independent contractors is the issue of 'control.' As a salaried minister of a church, the church exercises control over the majority of his or her services. The church has established days and hours of worship services, expecting the minister to lead these religious worship services. The church generally has established office hours of some form, expecting him or her to maintain regular office hours and see to the administrative and pastoral duties of the church. Because the church holds considerable control over the performance of the duties, most ministers with regular salaries from churches should be considered common-law employees. However, they are also considered self-employed for these earnings as well as for SECA purposes, thereby creating their "dual-status."

Most churches, then, should issue ministers a Form W2 at year-end, as opposed to a Form 1099-MISC.

Ministers are fully self-employed for such additional ministerial services as performing weddings or funerals for individuals. All such services performed outside the scope of work for the church are self-employment earnings and must reported as such on Schedule C of the Form 1040.

A Minister's W2

To properly prepare a minister's W2, a tax professional should understand what the church's basic payroll obligations are for ministerial staff.

---

[3]*Memo #12: Who Is a Minister for Tax Purposes?* Publication of Pensions and Benefits USA, Kansas City, Missouri.

Regarding social security taxes, ministers are always considered self-employed. For the church, this means that the church cannot withhold social security or Medicare taxes on its ministers. Ministers must pay their own SECA taxes, through one of two options to be discussed later, unless they have been approved for exemption (discussed later).

A common-law minister's salary and other federal taxable compensation must be shown in Box 1 of his W2. If his salary is also taxable to the appropriate state agency, the state taxable amount should be shown in Box 16, State taxable wages. Unless the minister chooses voluntary withholding or participates in a church-sponsored retirement plan, no other boxes of the W2 are usually required to be completed. Boxes 3, 4, 5, and 6 should never have any amounts reported by a church on a minister's W2. The only exception is in reference to a vow-of-poverty member as discussed earlier.

Box 12 may have items, if any are applicable. Box 14 may contain extraneous information, such as the minister's Housing Allowance (discussed later).

Withholding of Taxes on a Minister

For federal and state withholding requirements, they are considered employees and may have federal and state taxes withheld, depending on any voluntary withholding arrangement made with the church.

A minister is <u>not</u> subject to federal withholding requirements, as non-ministerial employees are. Therefore, the church <u>can only</u> withhold federal income taxes on its minister <u>if</u> there is a voluntary federal withholding agreement made between the church and the minister. Both must agree for this to be valid. To enter a voluntary withholding agreement with the church, the minister presents a Form W4 to his church.

If voluntary withholding is chosen, the church must pay and report the federal taxes withheld as required per Circular E and Form 941 or Form 944, whichever is applicable. Depending on the individual state's requirement, voluntary state withholding may or may not be allowed as well. The minister must comply with the governing regulations in his or her state and locality.

Please note that in no way may a church <u>pay</u> a minister's taxes <u>for</u> him. Some churches have erroneously paid the minister's half of his social security and Medicare taxes, misunderstanding their payroll obligations. When a church has mistakenly paid a minister's taxes on his or her behalf, then the minister's taxable federal compensation must be increased by this amount. This, of course, creates an upward spiral effect, as this now makes his tax liability for SECA and/or federal and state higher. As tax professionals, we do our churches and our ministerial clients a great service by educating them so they do not make this mistake.

If voluntary federal withholding is chosen, the minister can add an extra amount to help cover his SECA tax liability, if he desires. It must, however, be withheld as **federal income tax withholding** and added to Box 2 of his W2. It cannot be treated as "Social Security" or "Medicare" taxes.

If the minister is a vow-of-poverty member of a religious order, his earnings are considered the earnings of the order and are tax-free to him. Income he earns outside the order, however, may be considered taxable income and subject to federal and SECA taxation.

When a Minister Might Receive a 1099-MISC

Some churches have given their ministers a 1099-MISC instead of a W2. In many cases, this is an oversight and unintentional error on the part of well-meaning churches. Mostly this results from an ignorance of the payroll and tax reporting requirements for churches in regard to their ministerial staff. Keeping in mind that much of the financial and payroll reporting done by a church is done by volunteers may explain the ignorance of the pertinent laws and regulations.

However, there may be legitimate times when a minister receives a 1099-MISC instead of a W2. Examples could include a traveling minister who doesn't have a regular church but travels conducting religious worship services at a variety of venues throughout the year. At any one hosting church, if this minister receives compensation (including 'love offerings') that exceed $600, this minister should receive a 1099-MISC from that church as an itinerant minister.

If the minister works solely on his own and receives ministerial compensation (perhaps as a temporary pastor or traveling minister) throughout the year, he may need to be issued a 1099-MISC if his payment from one church or organization exceeds the $600 threshold for 1099-MISC.

In any case, the minister must report all his self-employment income on Schedule C, even if it is below the 1099-MISC threshold from any one organization. A minister should be responsible to record all income contemporaneously.

How a Minister Pays his Taxes
Unless voluntary withholding with the church is chosen (as described above), a minister must pay his own taxes through the estimated tax system. As is the case with other self-employed individuals, quarterly Form 1040-ES payments should be made and paid contemporaneously through the year. These are then shown on the Form 1040 as estimated tax payments.

Exemption from Social Security and Medicare

A minister can opt out of the public social security and Medicare system, one of the unique options available to him or her. To qualify, the minister must file Form 4361 no later than the due date (including extensions) of the tax return for the second tax year in which he or she had at least $400 of net earnings from self-employment (at least partly from ministerial services). The two years do not have to be consecutive years.

The minister may file if he or she meets the following additional requirements:

- Is conscientiously opposed to public insurance because of individual religious considerations (not because of general conscience), or is opposed because of principles of the religious denomination.
- Files for other than economic reasons.
- Notifies the church or order that he or she is opposed to public insurance (other than a vow-of-poverty member). This requirement does not apply to Christian Science practitioners or readers.
- Is ordained, commissioned, or licensed through a tax-exempt religious organization.

- Establishes that the organization is a church or a convention or association of churches.
- Did not make a previous election to be covered under public insurance
- Signs and returns the statement the IRS mails to the minister to certify that this exemption request is based on the grounds listed on the statement.

Once the IRS approves the exemption request, they will mail an approval notice. The minister should keep this as part of his permanent files. On the self-employment tax line of the Form 1040, the words "Exempt-Form 4361" will be printed or handwritten prior to submitting the Form 1040 to the IRS, and no SE tax with be calculated on his ministerial earnings.

Ministers should note, however, that this exemption _only_ applies to his self-employment ministerial earnings. He or she must still be responsible for self-employment tax on all non-ministerial, self-employment income. An example could be when a minister owns another business in addition to the ministerial services he or she provides for the church.

If the minister is a member of a religious order and <u>has taken</u> a "vow of poverty," his earnings are **already** exempt from SECA taxes. He does not need to file a separate exemption. Even in such a case, your earnings may be subject to FICA taxes, if the religious order has filed Form SS-16 and elected social security coverage for its current or future vow-of-poverty members. If the election is made by the order, it can revert back to twenty prior calendar quarters. The religious order, however, pays **both** the employer and employee's share of social security and Medicare taxes in this case.

If the minister is a member of a recognized religious sect, he can still apply for exemption. However, he or she would use Form 4029. In this case, the minister applies for exemption on self-employment income and on wages earned from an employer that has obtained exemption. The eligibility requirements vary somewhat from the requirements for ministers of churches, and these rules and instructions on filing Form 4029 can be found in IRS Pub 517, available on www.irs.gov.

Chapter Three

Reimbursements and Fringe Benefits

The tax treatment of any reimbursements paid to the minister, or any fringe benefits he or she receives, depends upon the type of plan they are paid under and the type of fringe benefits received.

Non-Accountable Plans vs. Accountable Plans

A church may reimburse its minister for various church-related expenses incurred by the minister in a similar way as a secular employer reimburses its employees. The tax treatment varies, dependent upon whether the reimbursement is given under an Accountable Plan or a Non-Accountable Plan.

For a church to have a qualified Accountable Plan, it must meet all of the following three conditions:

- The expenses must have a legitimate church business purpose, paid or incurred in the course of the minister's service as an employee of the church.

- The minister must adequately account to the church for the expenses within a reasonable period of time.
- The minister must return any excess reimbursement within a reasonable period of time.

This Accountable Plan should be a part of the church's official documents in writing. Any reimbursements that meet the above requirements will <u>not</u> be included in the minister's W2 taxable compensation amount.

Expense reports and mileage logs should be turned into the appropriate church staff within a reasonable period of time, usually within 30-45 days. A simple way to meet the "reasonable" time requirement is to have monthly expense reporting established. At the end of the month, the minister delivers the expense report, including mileage log, to the appropriate church staff, who in turn issues a reimbursement check shortly thereafter.

If the reimbursement equals the amount of the business expenses, no deductions for the minister result. If, however, the reimbursement is less than the business expenses, the remainder may be allowable on the minister's taxes as a reduction for SE tax purposes (explained later) and/or as deductible remaining unreimbursed business expenses.

If the reimbursement exceeds the amount of the business expenses, the excess must be returned to the church within a reasonable period of time, or it must be added into the wages reported in Box 1 of the W2.

A Non-Accountable Plan exists when reimbursements are paid and the plan does not meet the three requirements listed above for an Accountable Plan. All reimbursements paid through a Non-Accountable Plan are <u>added</u> to the W2 wages in Box 1. Because of this, all legitimate business expenses may be claimed as deductions on the minister's tax return for both SE and federal reporting purposes. The full amounts of these are then claimed as deductions on Form 2106 or Form 2106-EZ as well as on Form SE.

Tax Treatment of Minister's Mileage

In the course of his services as a minister, the use of his personal vehicle for church-related business means allowable business mileage. The minister must maintain a log of such miles in order for these to be deductible or excludable as a reimbursement.

As mentioned earlier, mileage paid under an Accountable Plan will not be included in the minister's taxable compensation as long as the reimbursement **does not exceed** the federal allowable standard mileage rate, as updated annually by the IRS. The church may reimburse at any amount they choose up to the allowable federal rate. Any difference between the rate the church reimburses and the federal standard mileage rate can be claimed by the minister on his Form 2106 (or 2106-EZ), and as a reduction in SE gross income calculations.

Any mileage reimbursed under a Non-Accountable Plan, which is included in Box 1 of the minister's W2, can also be claimed as a deduction on Form 2106 and as a reduction in SE gross income calculations, since the full amount was reported as taxable income on his or her W2.

Ministers should understand their responsibility to keep proper mileage records, including the dates, odometer readings, total business miles, and business purpose of each trip. These logs should be kept contemporaneously.

Should a church pay its minister a Car Allowance instead of requiring mileage logs, the minister should still keep and report mileage information. The difference between the Car Allowance paid the minister and the allowable mileage rates the minister should receive. The minister remains responsible to return any excess reimbursements, including those paid under an Accountable Plan. It is not generally recommended that churches issue Car Allowances of set amounts.

Whether a church issues a Car Allowance or not, the church must realize the responsibilities of matching the allowance given to the allowable amount as figured from the mileage records. Excesses must be returned to the church, under an Accountable Plan, or they must be added to the minister's W2 as taxable wages. Remember, any reimbursements paid under a Non-Accountable Plan are included in Box 1 of the W2 as taxable wages.

If the church owns the vehicle that the minister uses on a regular basis, the church may pay all the costs of the vehicle. However, the value of the minister's personal use of this vehicle must be added into his taxable compensation in Box 1 of his W2.

Housing, Rental, or Parsonage Allowances

Many churches offer housing allowances or parsonage allowances to their ministers. This is one way the church can help a minister with income taxes, so it's important for tax professionals to understand how this applies to a minister's tax return.

A housing (or parsonage) allowance can be given by a church to a minister separately from his "salary." Housing Allowances are generally given to ministers who own or rent their own homes. Parsonage Allowances, however, apply to ministers who live in a parsonage or other church-owned property, generally on a rent-free basis.

The housing allowance is <u>not</u> included in the minister's federal taxable compensation reported in Box 1 of his or her W2. It is, however, included for SECA purposes. For this reason, and knowing that the amount must be known for the minister's tax return to be completed correctly, it is advisable for churches to report the total amount given as Housing (or Parsonage) Allowance in Box 14 of his or her W2.

In order for a church to issue such housing allowances to its minister, the minister should complete a request form for the housing allowance totals. Richard Hammar's *Church & Clergy Tax Guide*, updated annually, or other resources, have sample forms showing all the items that ministers should include in the calculation for this request.

The minister should present this formal request to the church's governing board, whether a Board of Deacons, Elders, or other decision-makers for the church. This Board must then approve the minister's request.

Once the governing board has approved the housing request, the church may then divide the minister's salary package and issue this portion of his compensation as "Housing Allowance."

For example, if a church hires a minister for a total salary package of $50,000 per year, and a minister's estimated housing costs per his completed request total $20,000 for that year, the church may approve and designate $20,000 as "Housing Allowance" for the minister, leaving $30,000 to be treated as federal taxable salary. Instead of $50,000 in Box 1 of his or her W2, Box 1 now shows $30,000. The Housing Allowance can be noted in Box 14 with the amount of $20,000 printed there. This gives the tax professional the housing amount needed to properly calculate the SE earnings for this dual-status taxpayer.

It must be understood that an approval of a housing allowance for a minister must <u>always</u> be proactive. It can <u>never</u> be retroactive. Because of this, it is generally recommended that a minister present such request annually for the new year and prior to his first payday in that new year.

For ministers who live in church-owned property at a rent-free or discounted-rate basis, the church and minister should understand that a Fair Rental Value of this housing must be included in the minister's taxable compensation package.

For example, if Rev. A lives in the parsonage next door to ABC Church and pays no rent to the church, the church must consider the Fair Rental Value (FRV) of the parsonage as part of the pastor's total taxable package. This is similar to the Housing Allowance example earlier.

Keep in mind, however, that the minister's true housing costs exceed the FRV. He also has utilities, furnishings, repairs and maintenance, and other living costs, which should be allowed for his nontaxable housing allowance totals. Therefore, a church in this situation may have both a Parsonage Allowance to consider and a Housing Allowance for the remainder of his housing costs. Both should be treated as nontaxable for federal tax purposes, but remain taxable for SECA purposes.

Bear in mind also that, if the minister has deductible business expenses relating to his housing, the tax preparer must allocate between the portion attributable to taxable income and the portion attributable to tax-exempt income. A minister cannot deduct the portion allocable to the tax-exempt income (such as Housing Allowance).

IRS Pub 517 gives additional guidance on figuring this allocation, including invaluable worksheets to help guide you through the calculations. Worksheet 1 gives guidance on the allocations between taxable and tax-exempt income for the minister's income and housing allowances. Worksheet 2 helps the professional break down the allocations for Schedule C deductibility purposes. Worksheet 3 helps break down the allocations for Form 2106 reporting purposes.

Many churches have erred with the proper treatment of housing or parsonage allowances for their ministers, so tax professionals should educate their clients accordingly.

Fringe Benefits for Ministers
Retirement Options

A minister can contribute in a variety of ways into a retirement account to provide for future needs, as other individuals and employees can. Ways a minister can set aside funds for retirement include, but are not necessarily limited to, Section 403(b) plans, Section 457 plans, IRA's, and other qualified plans. Some of the same rules apply to certain retirement programs of his, or the church's, choosing.

Some rules vary, however. For example, for IRA's (Individual Retirement Accounts) a minister's housing allowance cannot be considered as part of his compensation for purposes of figuring his IRA contribution or deductibility.

If a minister is covered by a church or organization-sponsored plan, the Retirement Plan box on his W2 should be checked and the appropriate code listed in Box 12. The tax professional should make sure that all applicable rules are followed in the proper treatment of his retirement contributions and potential deductibility for these items. This topic is beyond the scope of this course.

Please bear in mind that, in many cases, if the minister meets all other eligibility requirements of the Retirement Savers Credit, the contributions he or she has made to such a retirement plan may quality for this credit. The tax professional should never overlook this benefit for the client.

Also, we tax professionals should always inquire as to any IRA's that the client has personally set up and is contributing into. In many cases, the same rules will apply for our clergy clients as for our other clients in terms of eligibility and deductibility of contributions. Please be aware that the housing allowances a minister receives may require different treatment and the tax professional should follow all applicable code regulations for this.

Car and Mileage Allowances

Car Allowances may be given by a church to its ministers and its tax treatment varies, dependent upon certain factors.

If a church pays a flat-fee amount of a car allowance and <u>does not</u> require a substantiation of mileage and repayment of any excess allowance figured therein, the **<u>entire</u>** allowance is considered taxable compensation to the minister and is added into Box 1 of the W2. He, then, can take a deduction for his business mileage on Form 2106/EZ, carrying to Schedule A.

If a church pays a flat-fee amount of a car allowance and <u>does</u> require a substantiation of mileage and repayment of any and all excess allowance figured therein, the allowance **is not** considered taxable compensation and **is not** included in Box 1 of the W2. This is only true if the minister fulfills his requirement to substantiate his mileage and repay any and all excess allowance within a reasonable period of time. He will not, in this case, be able to deduct these business miles on a Form 2106, without showing the total amount of the church's reimbursement for these miles as well.

A church may opt to pay its minister a mileage rate upon presentation of mileage logs, within a reasonable period of time, for all business miles. As long as this is paid under an **Accountable** Plan (referenced earlier), this method fulfills all the requirements concerning reimbursements of mileage, because:

- It demands substantiation of business miles and
- It causes the church to reimburse only for business miles, eliminating excess reimbursements.

In this way, none of the reimbursement is taxable compensation to the minister, <u>unless</u> it exceeds the allowable federal standard mileage rate for business miles. A church can opt to pay any rate up to the federal allowable rate. If a church chooses to reimburse below the federal allowable rate, the minister may deduct the difference between the federal rate and the rate of the reimbursement for those miles on Form 2106/EZ.

Any mileage reimbursements paid under a **Non-Accountable** Plan are considered taxable wages, added to Box 1 of the W2, and fully deductible on the minister's Form 2106/EZ.

Insurance

For ministers who are self-employed, they may be able to deduct the self-employed health insurance premiums they paid for health insurance.

Requirements to take these as a deduction include:
- The minister is self-employed.
- The payment is for medical, dental, and long-term care insurance for the minister, the minister's spouse, and the minister's dependents.
- The expenses taken into account for this exclusion are not deductible as medical

expenses on Schedule A, Itemized Deductions.

- The exclusion is not allowed for any month in which the minister is eligible to participate in a subsidized plan of the minister's (or of the minister's spouse's) employer.
- The exclusion cannot exceed the net earnings of the business under which this plan is established. This does <u>not</u> include common-law earnings from a church.

For 2010, these premiums may also be allowed as a reduction in the net earnings subject to SE tax for a self-employed taxpayer. This reduction may continue for future years. Current tax law should always be followed.

Chapter Four

Preparing the Minister's Tax Return

Once the tax professional obtains a W2 and any other pertinent documentation regarding the client's tax situation, the preparer can begin the preparation of the Form 1040 and its accompanying schedules.

W2 Wages

As with other clients, the Box 1 wages on the W2 of a common-law minister goes to Line 7 of the Form 1040.

Schedule C

For all self-employed ministers (as discussed above), the tax professional must complete a Schedule C. All gross receipts from the services provided (including love offerings) must be shown as gross income. All deductible expenses are broken out and listed as applicable on the Schedule C.

Common deductible business expenses for ministers include, but are not limited to:
- Business miles (discussed in detail earlier)

- Meals and entertainment, such as business lunches with other ministers or leaders for ministry-related purposes
- Travel expenses, such as ministry-related lodging or airfare
- Trade publications, dues and subscriptions relating to ministry
- Books and supplies for ministry
- Tax preparation and other professional fees
- Pastor's conferences and conventions

Office in Home Deduction

A taxpayer may be able to take an Office-in-Home deduction for the business portion of his or her home under certain conditions. These rules may, or may not, apply to ministers as well.

To qualify for an Office-in-Home deduction, a taxpayer must:
- Use the designated space in the home **<u>regularly and exclusively</u>** for business purposes, or
- As a place to meet and deal with customers, clients, or patients in the normal operation of their business, or
- In connection with a trade or business when there is a separate structure not attached to their home, or

- In operation of a home daycare facility, or
- As rental property, or
- As a place for regular storage of certain business items, such as inventory or product samples.

To determine if an Office-in-Home deduction is applicable to the minister, certain factors need to be determined. If the minister works as a common-law employee of the church and has an office provided at the church where he works from, the Office-in-Home deduction may not be available. The tax professional must investigate and make certain that the Office-in-Home requirements are truly met <u>before</u> allowing this deduction.

When a <u>common-law</u> minister has an office in the home, according to IRS Fact Sheet on the Home Office Deduction, the regular and exclusive use of the minister's home must be "for the convenience of their employer (the church)" and cannot be rented by the church. The tax preparer must make certain, in any case involving a minister, that a qualifying office in home deduction exists before allowing it.

If a minister, on the other hand, has no available office to work from and uses an office in his home as his primary business locale and meets the above-listed requirements, he can take an Office-in-Home deduction on either Schedule C (for self-employed ministers) or Form 2106 (for common-law employees).

Keep in mind that in either case, that of a self-employed minister or a common-law employee who otherwise qualifies, the use of the home office must be **both** **regular** and **exclusive**.

Form 2106 or 2106-EZ and Schedule A, Miscellaneous Deductions

For common-law ministers who have unreimbursed employee business expenses, or for under-reimbursed employee business expenses, the tax preparer should evaluate all such expenses and make the proper deductions for these.

It could be that a line item on the Schedule A, Miscellaneous Deductions Subject to 2% is completed to account for these. However, it may be necessary to complete Form 2106/EZ instead, the totals of which then carry to Schedule A, Miscellaneous Deductions Subject to 2%.

To complete the Form 2106/EZ and/or Schedule A, Miscellaneous Deductions Subject to 2%, take into account the following unreimbursed (or under-reimbursed) expenses the minister has incurred and paid through the year:

- Business-related meals and entertainment expenses
- Business-related travel and lodging, including airfare, car rentals, etc.
- Business-related professional books, journals, dues, and subscriptions
- Business-related professional conferences and continuing education that meets appropriate requirements
- Business mileage
- Other qualifying ordinary and necessary business expenses

Remember to account for reimbursements received by the employer which are not included in his W2 wages. The remaining amounts of unreimbursed expenses are then carried from Form 2106/EZ to Schedule A, Miscellaneous Deductions Subject to 2%. Remember to include in this section of Schedule A the tax preparation fees he or she paid in that year and other miscellaneous deductions that apply to this section as well.

Schedule A

Other sections of the Schedule A, Itemized Deductions may also apply to your minister. For example, the real estate taxes and mortgage interest he may have paid on his home can be itemized here. For a minister who has also been paid a Housing Allowance, which includes these costs, he or she **is still allowed** to deduct these on the Schedule A as legitimate itemized deductions. This process is known as "double-dipping" and is allowed for ministers in this case. It is a unusual tax benefit that ministers enjoy.

Remember to include any state income or state estimated income taxes paid by the minister in that year, as well as the minister's charitable contributions to 501(c)3 organizations, applying the limits as usual.

The minister may have qualifying medical insurance or other medical expenses to claim. Remember, however, that any premiums used in the calculation of the self-employed health insurance deduction **cannot** be included again in this section. Other medical, dental, and qualifying costs for health care may be included here.

Schedule SE

If the minister is self-employed for all his earnings, the Schedule C or C-EZ must be completed first. If the minister is a common-law employee of the church, although the Schedule C or C-EZ may not be completed, the Schedule SE will still need to be prepared.

Only if a minister has been approved for exemption from social security and Medicare taxes will a Schedule SE not be filed. Instead, on the SE tax line of the Form 1040 in the dotted line, the words "Exempt--Form 4361" will be printed.

To complete the Schedule SE, use either the short form or long form Schedule SE. In many cases, the minister can simply file the short-form Schedule SE on both his common-law employee ministerial earnings and his self-employment earnings. If the church has elected out of social security and you need to use long form Schedule SE, do not include the minister's income on Line 5a, as it is not considered church employee income.

To calculate the total amount to enter on Line 2 of either the short form or long form Schedule SE, you must include the following:

- W2 Box 1 federal taxable wages (which should include any <u>taxable</u> reimbursements or fringes)
- Housing or Parsonage Allowance
- The value of meals and lodging provided to the minister, the minister's spouse, or the minister's dependents for the church's convenience

Do not include on Line 2 of Schedule SE retirement benefits a retired minister receives from his or her church plan after retirement. Also, do not include a Housing or Parsonage Allowance provided to the minister by the church <u>after retirement</u>.

To properly arrive at the correct total on Line 2 of Schedule SE, you also need to subtract the minister's unreimbursed deductible business expenses (from Form 2106/EZ), which includes the minister's business mileage calculations. A statement should be included showing how the calculations for Line 2 were arrived at. Also, keep in mind that allowable housing-related business expenses must be reduced by the allocable percentage attributable to tax-exempt income (such as Housing Allowance).

Once Line 2 is calculated, and before entering the total on Line 3, adjust for any amount listed as an exclusion to AGI for the minister's self-employed health insurance premiums. The resulting total is the Line 3 amount, applicable to the SE tax. Complete Form SE and carry the SE tax to the appropriate line of the Form 1040.

Tax Credits

Be sure to evaluate what tax credits apply to this minister's tax situation. Possible credits include:

- Retirement Savers Credit for contributions to qualified retirement plans or IRA's
- Dependent Care Credit for children, if both spouses (on a Married, Filing Joint return) are gainfully employed
- Earned Income Credit (using the worksheets to modify the income as instructed and evaluate to see if qualifications are met)
- Child Tax Credit
- Additional Child Tax Credit
- Education Credits

The tax professional should evaluate every available credit for ministers, just as for all other clients, and give ministers all such benefits to which they are entitled.

Retired Ministers

If a minister is receiving retirement benefits from a church plan, these benefits may, or may not, be taxable to him.

If the retirement is paid to the minister as a "Rental Allowance" or "Housing Allowance," the minister can exclude this from his gross income. Depending upon the way the 1099R is printed and coded, the tax professional may need to attach a supporting statement to the return showing the qualifying exclusion from income.

1099R's that are for normal distributions after qualifying retirement are generally included in the gross income as usual. General rules pertaining to the treatment of retirement income are followed in this case.

****

About the Author

For more than 30 years, Kay K. Mortimer, EA, has enjoyed a career providing excellent and professional tax and accounting services. With her faithful staff of 24 years, Kay owned her own tax business serving approximately 2000 clients annually. During that time, she specialized in small businesses, churches, nonprofits and individuals' tax and accounting needs, including payroll and Quickbooks.

Kay has also taught tax professional CPE classes and webinars both nationally, regionally, locally and online. This compact ministers' tax guide is one of her products and is a result of her specialized experience serving churches and ministers for most of her career. As an Ordained Minister herself, she has unique insight into the tax and accounting needs of churches and ministers.

Since selling her business in 2013, Kay now enjoys part-time tax consulting work and concentrating on her full-time ministry and writing work as an Ordained Minister. She serves her local church and other Christians all over the world through Covenant Truth Ministries and its resources, teachings, and ministry. Find out more about Kay's ministry by visiting www.covenanttruthministries.com.